AND THE MIRACLE IS...

John F. Campoli

His Love Press
Allenhurst, New Jersey

Published by His Love Press
                P.O. Box 433
                Allenhurst, New Jersey 07711

Scripture Reference:
All Scripture quotations were taken from the HOLY BIBLE, NEW INTER-NATIONAL VERSION, Copyright © 1973, 1978, 1984 by International Bible Society.

Cover art by Candace Lynn Rathbone
ISBN 0-9625676-0-4

Dedication

I would like to dedicate this volume to my mother, the first person who taught me that miracles really do exist in our lives.

Acknowledgements

Special thanks to everyone who encouraged me to publish this volume. In particular, I am especially greatful to Chris Bhalla, Mary Buckman and Pat McCluskey who worked so hard in preparing the manuscript.

Contents

Author's Preface.................................ix

1. The Word..1

2. The Heart of Christ............................9

3. The Patience of the Lord......................15

4. To Be Fearless................................21

5. Strength and Trust............................29

6. The Good News and the Bad News...........35

7. We Can Walk on Water.........................41

8. We Have a Name...............................49

9. Always Being Ready...........................55

Epilogue...63

About the Author................................65

Author's Preface

"This salvation, which was first announced by the Lord, was confirmed to us by those who heard him. God also testified to it by signs, wonders and various miracles, and gifts of the Holy Spirit distributed according to His will." Hebrews 2:3a-4

God has a miracle for each and every one of us; all we have to do is reach out and claim that miracle, take it and make it our own. The miracle that God is holding out to us is that, two thousand years after the resurrection of Jesus Christ, miracles are still performed in His name each day. That in itself, is one of the greatest miracles.

Do you really believe in miracles? Do you believe they are happening in your life? Do miracles happen even if you don't believe in them? I believe miracles take place each and every day of our life, but because of a lack of faith, when they occur they go unnoticed and unclaimed. In Scripture there is one element underlining all the miracles of Jesus and that is faith.

When Jesus healed He usually told the person it was his faith that had healed him, his faith that had made him whole. Over and over again this theme is repeated throughout the Gospels. Jesus did not say it's the faith of your community. No, He said it's your faith that has made you whole, your individual, personal faith. That's what salvation is all about. It should never get too abstract, too removed. It's easy to say, "Oh, Jesus died for everyone, what does He care about me as an individual?" He did die for everyone, but He also died for you as an individual. He lives in you. He loves you so much. He has made a covenant with you, a covenant which promises He will never abandon you and He will answer all your needs, even if it takes a miracle.

In actuality, it is up to each one of us to work out our own personal salvation, which comes from an unconditional acceptance of Jesus as Lord and Savior of our lives. Once the acceptance of Jesus has been made we can expect that whatever is asked for in faith will be received. Jesus has promised that. In faith, miracles can be expected.

The following pages point out some of the great miracles in our lives — miracles which often go unnoticed — in the hope that our eyes will be opened to the fact that today, two thousand years after the time of Christ, He still performs miracles.

CHAPTER 1

. . . And the Miracle Is —
The Word

"All Scripture is God-breathed and is useful for teaching, rebuking, correcting and training in righteousness...." 2 Timothy 3:16

God has given us His inspired word to guide our life. The Bible is the beautiful love story of God's unbroken covenant with us.

God's chosen people were not always perfect — they were sinners — but God constantly called them to turn from sin and to surrender to Him. In the Bible, there are so many different accounts of people interacting with God. Who are these people? What did they feel? What did they think? Why did they act the way they did? These questions help the Bible come alive when it is being read.

In the Second Book of Kings we read the story of Hezekiah, an Old Testament king of Judah. What did Hezekiah do during his lifetime? What kind of a person was he? He was a man who had a conversion experience. Prior to this religious experience, he was a politician who wanted things for his own advantage.

The Jewish people of this time had allowed idolatry to creep into their religious practices. They worshiped the staff of Moses. It was an idol that took the place of God in their devotion. Hezekiah became aware that people were losing sight of God. As their king, he began to purify their religious observances. He trusted in the Lord and held fast to the Commandments. He gave his people the example of focusing everything on the Lord. The people of Judah worshiped at shrines on the mountain. Hezekiah had the sacred stones of the shrines smashed and shifted the focus to the temple in Jerusalem, making it the only place for worship. When studying the Scriptures, the significance of the temple and its meaning becomes apparent — the Temple is the dwelling place of God. Psalm 84 tells us that they are blessed, who dwell in God's house. It is also a refuge in times of trouble as we see from Hezekiah. (Is. 37:1) The temple, in the New Testament, refers to Jesus Christ. He is God dwelling on earth, our refuge in all our troubles.

Hezekiah became very ill. He was in the final stages of a terminal illness. He cried out to God for mercy and his plea was heard. God told Hezekiah, through the prophet Isaiah, ''I have heard your prayer and have seen your tears. I will cure you.'' (2 Kings 20:5-6) Isaiah ordered that a paste be made out of figs and applied it to the boils on Hezekiah's body. When this was done, he recovered.

Notice, Hezekiah had medical treatment as well as God's mercy. They both go hand in hand. God gives medicine to us. He gives wisdom to the doctors and wants us to use the medical help. It is foolish to say, ''I don't have to do anything because God is going to heal me.'' Yes, God does heal us, but God uses medicine and doctors as His earthly instruments. Remember that. God works His miracles. He grants His healing. He shows us in many ways that He is working signs and wonders in our lives. Take time to notice and to listen to God. Hezekiah was healed because of his faithfulness, his attempt to please God in his worship...his attempt to do God's will.

On the other hand, every time the Jewish people in their exodus from Egypt, turned to sin they wandered and wandered, as in the desert, further lost and further troubled. Their leaders would warn the people, "Be careful of the plagues and pestilences, of the destruction," but not "Be careful of your sins." It is the same thing today. All the major television stations warn us of impending disasters — hurricanes, floods, earthquakes, etc. — but they never mention sin. Every time the Jewish people turned from God, they were struck down. When they were faithful, God would feed and nourish them. God would protect them. He would lead them through their desert times with signs and wonders, just as He did Moses with the cloud. He is doing the same thing for us today — He is with us performing signs and wonders, sending us His angels to guide us each day. Too often, though, we are blind to them.

God seeks us always. He will never abandon us. His covenant with His chosen people is the same today as it was in the Old Testament. If we surrender to Him, He will always send us the help we need. It is true. Over and over in scripture we see this repeated. God made a covenant with us. He will never go back on it. We were called by Jesus Christ, we know Him, that is our gift. We are His. Jesus Christ is the answer to our problems. The minute we forget this, our problems become insurmountable. Jesus Christ, the Son of God, the Savior of the world, is the personal Lord and

Savior of each of us. The minute we lose sight of that fact, life loses meaning.

Who is Jesus Christ? He is the healer, He is the doctor, He is the one who helps us. He makes all our burdens light. He didn't come for those who have all the answers. He didn't come for the high and the mighty. He came for the poor, for the down-trodden, for the lonely. He came for the sinner. He came for you; He came for me.

To be a friend of Jesus when He walked the earth must have been very difficult. Just stop and imagine what it would have been like to be with Jesus. Try to visualize yourself living in that time. You are in the middle of nowhere, and yet in a moment there could be five-thousand people. You would be there scratching your head, wondering — He wants to feed all these people? It is impossible! How is He going to do that with just a few loaves of bread and some fish? What will He ask me to do next? Another day you go out with Him for a walk and you end up in a sinner's house, where you know you will be judged and condemned by everyone in the town. What are you doing talking to these people? Where will you spend the night? You ask Him and He says, "I don't have a place to lay my head, but you can lay right next to me on the ground here." What is your response? It had to have been difficult, trying to keep up with Him. Trying to guess what He was going to do next. How many times did the authorities try and stop Him? Every time they tried to throw stones at Him or tried to push Him off a cliff, He would just walk through their midst.

What if you were one of His disciples and stood there and saw all those rocks in their hands? How would you have felt? It wasn't easy to be with Jesus when He walked this earth. It is not always easy to walk with Him now.

We probably would not have understood His ways then, and we do not always understand His ways now. We never know when Jesus is going to call on us to be poor, or to be merciful. We never know when He is going to call on us to be humble, or to be compassionate. We never know when He is going to call on us to endure hardship in His name. In John's gospel Jesus tells us we must die to self. We must do the will of God on earth; that is our purpose for living.

Jesus died for us, He rose for us and because He rose for us we are all going to rise also. That's it! He is living in us and in those around us. God will heal us. He will heal each and every one of us if we accept it. He will heal us in the way that is most important in our lives. He will heal us by giving us salvation. The only way we can be assured of this healing is by saying, "Yes! Yes, Lord, you are the Way; I will walk the path you choose for me. I will take it no matter where you will lead me, because I know that if I walk with you — no matter how smooth or rocky the road, no matter how straight or how winding, no matter how many detours you might take — there is only one place you can lead me, and that is to the foot of the cross where you died for my sins so that I might live with you forever. In Jesus Christ all of us are glory bound.

HEZEKIAH'S CANTICLE OF PRAISE
UPON RECOVERING FROM HIS ILLNESS

I thought that in the prime of life I was going to the world of the dead, never to live out my life. I thought that in this world of the living I would never again see the Lord or any living person. My life was cut off and ended, like a tent that is taken down, like cloth that is cut from a loom. I thought that God was ending my life. All night I cried out with pain, as if a lion were breaking my bones. I thought that God was ending my life. My voice was thin and weak, and I moaned like a dove. My eyes grew tired from looking to heaven. Lord, rescue me from all this trouble. What can I say? The Lord has done this. My heart is bitter, and I cannot sleep.

Lord, I will live for you, for you alone; heal me and let me live. My bitterness will turn into peace. You save my life from all danger; You forgive all my sins. No one in the world of the dead can praise you. The dead cannot trust in your faithfulness. It is the living who praise you, as I praise you now. Fathers tell their children how faithful you are. Lord, you have healed me. We will play harps and sing your praise. Sing praise in your Temple as long as we live. Isaiah 38:10-20

CHAPTER 2

. . . And the Miracle Is —
The Heart of Christ

"Come to me, all you who are weary and burdened, and I will give you rest. Take my yoke upon you and learn from me, for I am gentle and humble in heart, and you will find rest for your souls."
Matthew 11:28-29

Many hearts are heavy because they bear sadness, grief and loss. All too often, after praying and praying, God hasn't answered our prayer in the way we anticipated. Still, with our heavy hearts we gather together to pray again and to plead with Him to hear us.

Jesus through His life, death, and resurrection, has taken all of our cares, all of our troubles, every problem — however real or imagined — to His own heart so that our broken hearts can be mended. He has taken all of our problems to the cross with Him, and He has left our problems crucified on the cross. He didn't take them with Him to glory. He didn't take them to the tomb with Him. He took them and left them there, on that cross at Calvary. It is true. Believe it and live as a healed, redeemed, glorified child of God. Don't hold back, look at Christ and see His love for us, allow that love to penetrate your heart.

When the love of God is blocked from our hearts, problems abound. This is the greatest obstacle to healing. If God is alive in us and life is lived for Him, all of our problems become instruments for His glory.

The only true problem is when we don't allow Jesus to live in us and to take over us. This removes love from our hearts. We might have emotions that appear to be love — one person here, one there, very selective — that's not love. That's not even the beginning of love. Jesus wasn't selective in His love for us. Jesus died just as much for the people that drove the nails into His hands, and those who raised Him on the cross, as He did for myself and anyone else who claims to be a Christian.

That's love! Loving everyone! Removing all traces of bitterness from our hearts. In order to love God and love others there can be no jealousy and no resentments in our heart. Take a tape recorder, turn it on and carry it for twenty four hours and see how many times uncharitable acts take place. How many times do our words pull another down instead of encouraging him to reach great heights? Where is the love? This would be a great spiritual exercise. It would take courage to play the recorder back. How many times in that twenty four hours was someone running somebody down, how many times were disparaging comments made, how many times was there spite? Was the truth about others told when it should not have been spoken? How often was honor given to God? Was it recognized that God lives in each person? Were demands and expectations placed on others? How many times was someone judged? To be unloving to each other is truly an offense against God. Believe that! The most important healing, is a healing of the heart.

To have the heart of Jesus living within us should be our ultimate desire. His heart loves all people, without exception. His heart contains no bitterness, no resentments, no hatred. Paul writes in his letter to the Corinthians, that many are sick and dying because they don't recognize the Body of Christ. (1 Cor. 11:29-31) We are God's children, we are the Body of Christ. Sinfulness breaks His heart.

When God created us, He created our bodies as perfect healing machines. Our bodies can heal themselves. It is helpful to use medicine but the essential components in healing are love and a positive attitude toward life.

To become well it is necessary to love God, our neighbor and ourselves. It is so important to understand this. In order to love God, it is necessary to love one another, and to love one another it is necessary to love ourselves; it is all interconnected. So many of us find it easy to say we love God and our neighbor but we often feel that self-love is selfishness. Selfishness is self-destructive. Self-love is simply accepting ourselves as the person God created. When He created us He saw that we were good and we should view ourselves in the same way. Jesus emphasized this when He said the two greatest commandments were to love God above all and to love our neighbor as ourselves (Mk. 12:31).

This is the choice: choose to be well or choose to be sick, choose to live or choose to die. People who live without love in their hearts are just existing. They are not living. To be truly alive is to live the life of Jesus Christ here on earth. Each moment of our life should be a witness of our belief in Him. That is the miracle — the peace, the contentment and the joy that fills the heart of the person who is living the life of Jesus, the life of love.

CHAPTER 3

. . . And the Miracle Is —
The Patience of the Lord

"Know therefore that the Lord your God is God, He is the faithful God, keeping His covenant of love to a thousand generations of those who love Him and keep His commands." Deuteronomy 7:9

We are the product of God's creation which leads me to believe that God either has a very strange sense of humor or He is ultimately patient. So often we come together and we proclaim that we believe Jesus Christ is our Lord and Savior. We proclaim that we are a saved and a forgiven people, that we have the right to the healings that God holds out to us, and yet so often after we've done all of these things, we say, "I'm still not healed." Why? Why aren't each and every one of us healed? It is not because God doesn't want to grant the healing. The problem is we place obstacles, major obstacles to healing in our lives.

We gather as a community to pray for healing and yet we go home and we hang on to our illness, not really believing we could be healed. We begin the organ recital...my head hurts, my back hurts, my kidney hurts, my heart aches. We go through the litany of all of our organs as if we were holding a recital. Our pain and our problems seem worse than everybody else's. We hang on to them, it is easier to do that than to let go. I know people who have asked God to heal them, have followed the doctor's regimen, been told by the doctors that their illness is going away, and then what do they do? At the first ache or pain they say, "I'm not really healed. God hasn't listened to my prayer." Before they know it, they've talked them-

selves right back into being ill. We keep reminding ourselves of our illness. We haven't given it up. We
haven't claimed the healing that God gave us. We
haven't even allowed it to work, because we don't
want to let go of it. We pray for healing and if we
would not put up obstacles we would feel the Spirit
going through us, touching us. In our hearts we cry
out, "Oh, I hope God heals me." What does that
mean, we hope that God heals us? He did! The minute we say we hope He did, we are saying, "I don't
really think He did." Why do we do that? Do we feel
unworthy of healings? We don't take the authority that
Jesus has given each and every one of us over the pow-
ers and forces of this world. We could force ourselves
to live like that forever. As long as we belong to the
organ recital club, we have blocked healing in our lives.

In order to have healing we must have faith. Over
and over in the Bible Jesus points out that faith causes
things to happen. We must have faith in God and in
His creation, ourselves. We must believe it in our heart
and not just give lip service.

Often we say, "Christ is Lord and Savior of my life,
I believe He has forgiven me, I believe I am reborn in
Him." If we mean this we cannot in our next breath
say, "Oh, I'm not worthy of anything." We must believe we are worthy of everything, if we are reborn in
Jesus Christ. We are worthy of the ultimate reward,
Heaven. We are good because we are forgiven. Surely,
there are going to be times in our lives that we are going to fall, but all we have to do is call out to the Lord
Jesus and before we even get the words out of our
mouth, we are all forgiven.

Another example of the patience of God is that He continues to love us in spite of the fact that we foolishly run after other gods without even realizing what we are doing. We proclaim that Jesus Christ is Lord and Savior and then we pick up the daily paper to read our horoscopes or we wear our little Italian horn around our neck to keep the devil away. If we really believe Jesus Christ is Lord and Savior of our lives, then we know that all that other stuff is garbage. We claim we do it for fun. Do we?

Another obstacle to healing is the thought that we all have to suffer in this life. Paul is often quoted to substantiate that idea. When Paul talks about the thorn in his side, he is not referring to an infliction of ill health; if that was the case, he could never have done the things he did. If we read this passage, we find that the thorn refers to temptation by the devil. (2 Corinthians 12:7) We often say, ''Oh, I have to bear my suffering.'' No, you don't. Jesus Christ bore your suffering. ''Oh, I'm going to offer my suffering as glory to God.'' Don't bother, because God doesn't get any glory out of your pain. God is not sadistic, God only gets glory when you are healed and you proclaim His glory and power. That is when God gets the glory, not through your suffering, not from your pain and your illness.

Scripture tells us Jesus came to heal and save. Salvation came with a cross, and through the power of this cross we have forgiveness for our sins. Don't forget that. God gave us the authority over evil in our world. We all have that authority. A beautiful Scripture passage is the parable where Jesus tells us, ''*Which of you, if his son asks for bread, will give him a stone? Or if he asks for a fish, will give him a snake?''* (Matt. 7:10) Then Jesus tells us that if we know how to give our children the right things, how much more will God give us the right things? He is telling us that He loves us and has given us the power over the evil one. Pray and accept the healings that Jesus offers you. Act in faith. Don't put your faith in psychics or horoscopes or crystals or anything else. Put your faith in Jesus Christ. Help your faith to grow and healing will follow. Read Scripture, listen to God's word proclaimed, allow it to come alive — live it. The more we know God the more we will grow in His image. If we can't do that first and foremost then all the rest of our prayers for healing, all the rest of our crying out means nothing, because we are still going to be where we were before. Accept Jesus as Lord and Savior of your life and mean it. Step out in faith and open yourself to the world that He has won for you, and that is Eternal Life with God the Father.

CHAPTER 4

. . . And the Miracle Is —
To Be Fearless

"Surely God is my salvation: I will trust and not be afraid. The Lord is my strength and my song: He has become my salvation." Isaiah 12:2

Fear is probably the most crippling, the most devastating emotion that can enter into the life of any person. No one is free from being attacked by fear, but when we allow ourselves to rest in Jesus Christ we can be assured that we will never be overcome by fear. When we trust in God we are not only able to overcome our fears, we are able to carry on our lives in peace.

Once there was a man who was out walking in the woods. He went a little too close to a ledge causing the ground to give way and he went tumbling down into a ravine. He reached out and he grabbed on to the branch of a tree which was growing out of the side of the ravine. He clung to the branch, helpless to reach safe ground; he became filled with panic. Below him were jagged rocks and he knew if he let go he would be dashed to death. He cried out, "Is there anybody up there? Somebody please help me!" He kept shouting over and over, then he started to pray. "Oh God! Help me! Help me! I don't want to die, I don't want to fall down. Oh God, do something! Help me!" Suddenly, God's voice came out of a cloud, "Do not be afraid, my son, I will help you, I will take care of you. In Scripture, I promised that I would send my angels to guard you and upon their hands they will bear you up; all you have to do is surrender to my will. (Psalm

91: 11-12) Now, let go; I will save you.'' The man hesitated a moment, then with all his might he hollered out, ''IS THERE ANYONE ELSE UP THERE WHO CAN HELP ME?'' Although this story is very humorous it is also very realistic. We probably would react the same way. We all have written the scenario on how our life should be unfolding and then when God has a different plan...we panic. How many times do we trust Him explicitly? If God were to tell us directly to let go, that He would provide for us, would we be willing to do so or would we still be too afraid? Would fear overwhelm us? I think most of us would probably be crying out with the man, ''Is there anybody else out there who can help me?'' We like the idea of having our feet on sure ground. Accepting the unknown is placing trust in God, but the fear of the unknown is probably the greatest fear that overcomes us. God realizes that.

In Luke's Gospel, in the story of the Annunciation, the angel told Mary she was to become the Mother of the Savior. Mary must have been afraid of the unknown. She knew that once she said ''yes'' her life would never be the same. The angel said, *''Rejoice, oh highly favored daughter, the Lord is with you.''* The idea of an angel appearing to her, a messenger from God asking such a special favor, was an awesome reality. The angel reassured her, *''Do not be afraid, Mary; you have found favor with God.''* (Lk. 1:28-30) God is with you. Put your trust in Him, and you have nothing to worry about.

Fear can cause us so many problems, especially a

fear of the unknown. Sometimes there is an illness in a family which occurs over and over, cancer, for example. A person in that family keeps saying, "I am going to die of cancer, I know it, everyone else did." They spend their whole life being afraid of cancer. They are so frightened that even if they were to have a sign that they had it, they would never go to the doctor. They say they don't want to know and therefore they don't get the help they need to avoid it. They are so filled with fear of the unknown that they bring the illness upon themselves.

Another example of this is the person with a history of heart disease in their family. They say, "Every man in my family died of a heart attack by the time they were forty years old." They get to be thirty-nine and a half and then they don't even have fingernails left; no, they don't even have fingers left. They have bitten them away with their worries and their fears. By their fortieth birthday their blood pressure is so high that they have a stroke and die. It happens so often. Once again the fear of what might happen becomes a self-fulfilling prophecy. Fear is most irrational and useless because what we think might happen in the future rarely does.

Another fear is a fear of people. We are afraid of what they can do to us. Will they say things about us to hurt us? Are they going to accept us? Are they going to like us? Remember, people cannot take hope away from us. People cannot take true love away from us. People cannot control us unless we allow it. There is nothing to be afraid of in another person.

There is the fear of places and things. Sometimes we don't even know what we are afraid of, we just feel frightened. We are afraid of heights, we are afraid of airplanes, we are afraid of elevators, we are afraid of escalators, we are afraid of old houses out in the woods, we are afraid of a lot of places. Places have no power over us. Millions of people ride airplanes every day and they don't get killed and they don't die, so why should we think that we are going to be the one who is going to die? It's the same with elevators, escalators, etc. It's the same thing as being in the room with the lights out — there is nothing to be afraid of. In reality most of the things we fear exist only in our imaginations.

Fear of the future paralyzes many people. There really is no such thing as the future. When it arrives it is today again. The past is over and it doesn't exist anymore. The here and now is the only thing that exists.

A now that is free from fear is a now that is peaceful and productive and useful. Years ago I read a verse which I have tried to make a part of my life. Whoever the author might have been gave advice that I think is timeless. It went something like this: yesterday is but a dream, tomorrow a vision, but today well lived, makes every yesterday a dream of happiness and every tomorrow a vision of hope. Instead of fearing for our health in the future, we should take care of our health today. If we fear for our family in the future, we must provide for them today. Then when that future "today" comes, they will be provided for. If I am going to be sick next year it won't do me any good to be worrying about it right now; because if I'm going to be sick next year, even if I'm going to die next year, worrying about it today is not going to change the fact. If I'm doing something wrong that is making me ill, I can change. I don't have to continue to do these things.

Jesus said when He was talking to Jarius, *"Fear is useless, what is needed is trust."* (Lk. 8:50) That is what He is calling each of us to have now — trust in Him! Trust doesn't mean being irrational and saying that God is going to take care of everything, that you don't have to do anything. It promises that if you give your day to God — truly give it to Him — all your actions are effortless. He will take over and do things so His plan here on earth is free to unfold! We pray the Our Father, "...Your kingdom come, Your will be done...," giving our day to the Lord, allowing Him to live in us, thus enabling His will to be done on earth. Whenever we trust in God, our inheritance is eternal life — with the hope of resurrection, of everlasting life, of that eternal glory that Jesus has called us to.

CHAPTER 5

. . . And the Miracle Is —
Strength and Trust

"Those who hope in the Lord will renew their strength. They will soar on wings like eagles; they will run and not be faint." Isaiah 40:31

We are on a spiritual journey. Each and every one of us are called to walk with Jesus Christ along the path of holiness. All life is a journey from the moment of conception until we enter the gates of eternal life.

If we look to Scripture we read about Abraham, seventy-five years old, a fine young man by the standards of some and an old man by the standards of others. (Genesis 12) Nonetheless, seventy-five years old, born and raised in the same place, very content and complacent. All of a sudden God tells him to pack up his family and move to another land. Abraham obeys God and moves. He doesn't know where he is going, but he knows God told him he had to go. He obeys.

In another Scripture passage we find Moses living in Egypt. (Ex. 3) God speaks to Moses and tells him he must lead his people out of Egypt and take them to the Promised Land. Moses obeys. Moses knew where he was going and was probably very excited. It didn't work out quite the way Moses expected...the journey lasted forty years and Moses never reached his final destination.

Jesus journeyed for three years. He performed miracles and He taught the people how to love and how to live. Jesus' journey led Him to a hill where He was

nailed to a cross. His journey led to persecution, suffering, pain and finally death. Jesus' journey did not
end at the cross; because of His obedience to the Father
the cross became the gateway to resurrection from the
dead into glory.

These are just a few examples of life's journeys.
Everyone who was ever created journeys toward eternal life, making decisions which will either bring them
closer to glory or leave them wandering, as Moses' people did in the desert. How many times do you go some-
where and you aren't sure where you are going or
what is going to happen? You sometimes wonder,
"Where am I going in life? Where will this lead me?
What will happen next?" You don't know. Sometimes
you think you know where you're going and it just
doesn't work out. You think you are following the
Lord's plan and suddenly it doesn't work out and you
must go off in another direction. How many times do
you think life is nothing but pain, sorrow, tribulation
and suffering? Many people feel that way about life.

Take care on the journey. There are many forks in
the road. Don't follow the road sign that reads "Why
me, poor me, always me." When we are walking with
Jesus it is impossible to talk like that. Jesus suffered
for you and me. Our pain from the trials and tribula-
tions we have here on earth is not like His. His pain
brought salvation to the world. Our pain can lead to
self-pity unless we are careful. The disciples, as they
walked with Jesus on His journey, had a glimpse of
the glory that was waiting for them. Jesus led them
up the mountain where He was transfigured before

them. His glory was so manifest that Peter exclaimed, "Lord, how good it is for us to be here." (Mk. 9:5) Nevertheless, when Jesus walked up that hill of Calvary most of His disciples didn't walk with Him — they ran away, they hid. The journey was becoming too rough for them.They were too frightened to take a chance. They didn't trust enough. They hadn't yet received the power of the Holy Spirit.

We are all given little glimpses of glory. Each time we experience happiness and peace we've had a glimpse of glory. We all have our moments, and these are necessary so we can know that the journey is worthwhile. Jesus wants you to take that walk with Him. He is calling you to do His will. Your walk with Him will take you up a hill, and there will be a cross on top of that hill — but you don't have to be crucified. He did that for you. The cross is only a wayside point. You will go past that cross and go on to the empty tomb. The journey with Jesus doesn't stop at the cross or at the empty tomb. Jesus' journey will take you and I to glory if we follow Him.

Life is a journey toward holiness. Take the fear and all the negative thinking out of your life. Cast it away and walk with Jesus. He is leading us to glory. He rose from the dead so that we could have life...life to the fullest. If we take the negative thinking that is locked within us and turn it into positive thinking, even our problems will give glory to God.

Jesus said if our faith was the size of a mustard seed, we could make the mountains get up and jump into the sea. If our faith was half the size of a mustard seed we would never have an ache or a pain, a problem or a worry. Jesus didn't tell us wait until you get out of this life and then you are going to glory. No, He died so that we could have a full life right now. Throw away the negatives in your life and accept His healing touch. Take a journey away from the negative to the positive. It brings healing. Accept the Spirit of Jesus Christ.

Paul reminds us that *"The fruit of the Spirit is love, joy, peace, patience, kindness, goodness, faithfulness, gentleness and self-control."* (Gal. 5:22-23) The Spirit that we receive is the Spirit of life. The Spirit upholds every bit of hope. When we truly accept Jesus as Lord and Savior of our lives the fruit of the Spirit will be manifest in us. That is what God is calling us to do and that is where our journey should be leading us. We journey away from negative ideas to the positive fact that we have all healing, all power in Jesus Christ. Give Him the glory and give Him the honor forever.

CHAPTER 6

. . . And the Miracle Is —

The Good News and the Bad News

"Then Jesus said to His disciples, 'If anyone would come after me, he must deny himself and take up his cross and follow me. For whoever wants to save his life will lose it, but whoever loses his life for me will find it. What good will it be for a man if he gains the whole world, yet forfeits his soul? Or what can a man give in exchange for his soul?' " Matthew 16:24-27

There was a man who was an avid golfer. One day an angel appeared to him and said, "I have some good news and some bad news for you. The good news is that heaven has the greatest golf course you could ever hope to play. The bad news is that you tee off in ten minutes." All of life is good news/bad news. The bad news for us (thought we'd better get the bad news out of the way first) is the fact that Jesus told us we have to carry our cross.

All followers of Jesus Christ carry a cross. Our crosses can be our backaches, headaches, heartaches and the pain, suffering and agony of just being human. Without a cross our conversations would be limited. We love to talk about our problems; that is the major topic of conversation among most people. That is the bad news.

The good news is Jesus tells us we only have to carry our cross, we don't have to get crucified on it. He already did that for us. We tend to think that all the crosses in our lives are leading to crucifixions, but there was only one crucifixion for our salvation. There was only one Person that was nailed to the cross for the salvation of each and every one of us. That person is Jesus Christ. That is a great miracle.

Every time I hear the Scriptures talking about carrying the cross, I'm reminded of the story of the man who, like all of us, had a cross that he had to carry in his daily life. I don't know what his cross was but I do know that he detested it. He complained and prayed so much that his cross would be taken away that God finally lost patience. He called St. Peter to Him and said, ''Peter, for my sake, I want you to do something about that guy down there, he's complaining about his cross, I can't stand his complaints anymore. Go down to the storeroom where we keep all the crosses and let him choose a new one.'' It seemed like a wonderful solution. St. Peter approached the man and said, ''Come with me. You're complaining so much about your cross God wants you to exchange it for a new one. As a follower of Christ you must carry a cross, but this time we are going to let you pick out your own.'' The man was overjoyed. He knew the cross he had now was worse than anyone else's. Great! He would be rid of it! Peter took the man up to the storeroom and took his cross and set it aside. It felt terrific not having to carry that heavy cross anymore. He started trying on different crosses. He picked up the first one and he couldn't even move it, and so he dropped that one right away. He picked up another one and he tried it on. It didn't seem too bad, it wasn't too heavy. As he started to move around he realized it was way too long, and it dragged along the ground. He picked up another one and it was too short, it jabbed him in his back every time he moved. This was getting ridiculous.

Over and over he tried different crosses and finally he found one that felt pretty good. It wasn't too heavy, or too long or too short. It even had a groove on it; it seemed to fit right on his shoulder. He turned to Peter and said, "I finally found a cross I can carry." Peter answered, "Believe it or not, it is the one you put down when you came into the room."

Stop and think about it. If we all threw our crosses in a pile and had to choose another we probably would reach for our own. We are familiar with the cross that we have in life. It becomes bearable by the very fact that we have grown used to it.

A person who is deaf feels his cross is awful and then sees someone who is blind. He watches them trying to manipulate. It's very difficult. He feels good that he can see to lip read. He can at least communicate and get around. He decides not to trade handicaps. The cross of cancer and the agony of chemotherapy makes the arthritis in someone's hands and back seem bearable. Yet, the person with the cancer going through chemotherapy treatments feels blessed when they see someone totally laid up with a completely debilitating handicap that gives them no life at all. They can't even move, and the chemotherapy doesn't seem so horrible. Even though I don't recommend that you compare your life with others, I do feel that when you look around you can always find somebody that has a worse cross than you.

The good part of carrying our cross in this life is that we don't have to get nailed to it, we don't have to die on it. Jesus died on the cross for all of us. He rose from the dead. He overcame death and He gave us new life. We don't have to do that; because of Jesus we will never face eternal death. Christ gives us life, life here on earth and everlasting life! The reality is that when we finish carrying our cross, when we finally lay it down for the last time, we are going to walk into glory with the Lord Jesus Christ. That is the greatest healing that we can ever have, knowing that we are going into glory, and that the cross we carry is the key to glory. We know this and we know that God loves us. He loves us and all He asks is that we love Him back.

When the Lord gave the Commandments to Moses He told him of His love for us and His desire for us to love Him in return. (Dt. 5:10) That is all that He asks of us. Jesus was the ultimate expression of God's love for us. If we accept that love, we have the final healing — everlasting life. Take the love He has for us, take the love of God and make it part of you. Allow that love to flow through you, to flow out to your parents, your friends, your family, to everyone you come in contact with. When the love becomes a part of you it appears like a soft hum that flows all around, changing the environment — it is here, it is there. This beautiful humming of love is so subtle, it lightens our burdens, it causes us to not only cease complaining about our cross but it enables us to carry our neighbor's. This love brings all healing, it brings Jesus so close we can see Him as He lives in each one of us.

CHAPTER 7

. . . And the Miracle Is —
We Can Walk on Water

" 'Lord, if it's you,' Peter replied, 'tell me to come to you on the water.' 'Come,' He said. Then Peter got down out of the boat, walked on the water and came toward Jesus. But when he saw the wind, he was afraid and beginning to sink cried out, 'Lord, save me!' Immediately Jesus reached out his hand and caught him. 'You of little faith,' he said, 'why did you doubt?' " Matthew 14:28-31

In Matthew's Gospel we have that beautiful account of Peter walking on the water to Jesus. (Mt. 14:22-23) It is a story of faith and healing. Picture how frightened the disciples must have been when the storm was raging. Jesus knew there was going to be a storm when they were out on the lake. It was necessary to teach them about faith. What did Jesus do? He went up on a mountain to pray. He was looking down on them in their little boat. The storm came up and they became upset and nervous. They thought they were going to drown. Jesus knew they needed to confront their fears and anxieties. He knew there was no danger of drowning from the water, but their fear and anxiety could certainly drown them. The storm raged, becoming more and more frightening. The disciples must have asked, ''Why is this happening?'' They were paralyzed with fear.

It happened then and it happens now. When fear overwhelms us we cease to live. We wander through the motions of living, walking the earth like the living dead. We wander around with fear, anxiety and depression. We no longer have life but we merely exist day after day. So often this is our first reaction when we are caught in the midst of a storm in our life. Why is this happening? We wonder if we displeased God in some way and brought about this punishment, this pain, this suffering. Was it our fault?

Other times we turn it around and say the devil is doing it. It would be great if all the world's problems could be blamed on him, but face it, he is not the cause of each and every problem that we have. When we start blaming him for everything we lose sight of the fact that we are the cause of some of our problems. When we start blaming him for everything we often forget the fact that we can help ourselves. When we start blaming him for everything we lose sight of the fact that Jesus died and rose to conquer sin and death.

Sometimes when things go wrong we claim Jesus doesn't care. We are being tossed, we are being drowned, we are losing it, we are losing our lives because Jesus doesn't care. He sent us out in the boat. He told us to go out in this storm. He doesn't care about us. I'm sure some of the disciples felt that way.

The disciples had seen everything that Jesus did up to the point of sending them out into the boat. They saw Jesus taking care of other people's needs. They had just come from witnessing the miracle of the multiplication of the loaves and fishes. They had seen great signs and wonders. They saw Jesus heal the sick, turn water into wine, and even raise the dead to life. They saw all these wonderful miracles when they were walking around with Him. They knew what He was doing for other people but they didn't know if He would do it for them?

When the storm came did they see Him? No. Even when He walked on the water, they thought he was a ghost, they didn't recognize Him. They started to cry out in fear, and fear was their greatest problem. They would drown because their fear and anxiety prevented them from seeing the presence of Jesus in their storm. It must have been a different ghost that each one of them saw. The ghost of their own insecurities, of their own sense of unlove, of their own unworthiness. Those were the ghosts they saw. That's what they felt, and they could not imagine why Jesus would save them.

Peter, the impulsive Apostle, sees Christ and climbs out of the boat and starts to walk across the water. All of a sudden he realizes what he is doing and he can't believe it — then he starts to sink. It's true. The minute he took his eyes off of Jesus and began to think he was in control fear struck him and he sank. When Jesus boarded the boat the storm ended. Wow! They were astonished at His power. They were so overwhelmed and so happy. They gave God praise and glory.

In our lifetime many storms buffet us. It might be the storm of a troubled relationship, a broken heart, a lost job, or an illness like cancer or AIDS. There are so many storms that engulf us and make it difficult for us to focus on Jesus. We must remember Jesus is with us always. He will help us through everything. We mustn't be blind to Him and the help He sends us because of fear.

We must take up our cross but we must remember that Jesus didn't carry His cross alone. Simon helped Him. That's a good lesson for us. It is necessary for us to be there for each other. This reminds me of a story I heard a long time ago about a little boy who was very frightened by a thunder storm. Each time the thunder would clap he would run to his mother for help. She was busy fixing dinner and so would pat him on the head and tell him to pray to God for courage. He would return to the other room and the thunder would sound again and he would run back to his mother. By the third time this was repeated the mother in frustration said, "Didn't I tell you to pray?" The little guy looked up in dismay and said, "Don't you know I need Jesus in the skin?" We all feel this way very often and so we must try to be Jesus in the skin for each other. We should not try to carry our cross by ourselves. He knows we can't make it alone.

When we are in pain, when we are in fear, when we are in anguish, it is very difficult to remember that Jesus is there on the mountain watching us and that He can and will supply all our needs. We don't need to be afraid that we are going to drown.

Once we have taken away the fear of drowning in the storm, the few waves that splash over the side of the boat will not matter. We all go to the amusement park and we love to ride the white river rapids, where the water splashes over us. We get a thrill because we know we are going to be safe. The storms in life can be a joy ride too, if we realize Jesus is there watching us and that nothing is going to happen. Nothing is going to harm us. If we take that attitude and really concentrate on Jesus watching over us providing all of our needs, then life's problems become a means of salvation. Believe me, we can endure, we can bear whatever it is we face in this life, however severe the storm. Jesus is there.

CHAPTER 8

. . . And the Miracle Is — We Have a Name

"But now, this is what the Lord says — He who created you, O Jacob, He who formed you, O Israel; 'Fear not, for I have redeemed you by name; you are mine. When you pass through the waters, I will be with you; and when you pass through the rivers, they will not sweep over you. When you walk through the fire, you will not be burned; the flames will not set you ablaze. For I am the Lord, your God, the Holy One of Israel, your Savior.'' Isaiah 43:1-3a

What does it mean to have a name? What does a name imply? We have a family name and our family name tells everybody who our relatives are, who our parents are. It gives us a dimension. We have a first name, the name which says who we are in the family. Together, our first and last names tell the world who we are.

God has called each and every one of us by name. In the earliest days of creation, when you named something you had control over it. That is why, we are told in the first book of the Bible, the story of creation, that when God created the heavens and the earth and all of the animals He put all of the creatures before Adam so that he could name them. (Gen. 2:19-20) This was a sign that God's supreme creation on this earth, had authority over all the earth and its creatures. God gave Adam and Eve authority over all the earth. (Gen. 1:28-30) God gave each of us a name which demonstrates that He has authority over us.

When God appeared to Moses in the burning bush Moses asked God, "What is your Name? Who are you?" God answered, *"I am who I am"* (Ex. 3:14-15) He is the one who is, the one who has existed before all times and will continue to exist. Moses was so over- come by the power of God's name that he wouldn't even utter it because he knew that would imply a certain authority on his part. Today if you pick up Jewish writings, you will never see the word God spelled out. All through Scripture, the writers never use the word God, they use Lord, Mighty One, Holy One, because of the reverence accorded a name.

Jesus Christ has given us His name, to use in authority and power. *"At the name of Jesus every knee should bow, in heaven and on earth and under the earth, and every tongue confess that Jesus Christ is Lord."* (Ph. 2:10-11) In the power of that name we can have anything that we need. In that name we can have everlasting life.

In the Acts of the Apostles we have the very beautiful account of Peter and John walking into the temple precincts where they meet a cripple who is begging. The cripple is telling them that he needs money. They tell him, *"Neither silver nor gold do I have to give you, but what I do have to give to you, is the name Jesus Christ, now stand up and walk."* (Acts 3:6) In the power of that name the man stood up and walked. For 2000 years Christians have been praying in the name of Jesus, and with the authority of that name miracles have occurred throughout the world. The name of Jesus is the name for healing. God has called each of us by name and He has authority over us, but He has given us the name of Jesus Christ so that we can take authority in our world. We can transform and renew the world and we can turn the world into the image of Jesus Christ here on earth. It is up to us. It is up to us to take and to make Jesus Christ the Lord and Savior of our life. It is up to us to make His presence known and felt in the world. Jesus tells the disciples and He tells us, *"Do not be afraid of those who kill the body and after that can do no more. But I will show you whom you should fear: Fear him who after killing the body, has power to throw you into hell. Yes, I tell you fear him."* (Lk. 12:4-5)

We must not fear the natural world. We need to be bold in the use of the name of Jesus Christ, and to realize that in that name we have authority. In that name we have power. In that name we have everything. In that name God has called us to life.

At Baptism we become one with Christ, we put on Christ, we become His presence in the world. Christ is calling us to be His body. If Christians throughout the world would only take the authority of His name, then we would renew the face of the earth. We could stand together and say The Lord's Prayer proclaiming the desire to have His kingdom come on earth — and see it happen. If we would surrender all to Him, we will have accepted the Covenant. As the author of Hebrews reminds us, *"This is the covenant I will make with the house of Israel after that time, declares the Lord. I will put my laws in their minds and write them on their hearts. I will be their God, and they will be my people. No longer will a man teach his neighbor, or a man his brother, saying, 'Know the Lord,' because they will all know me, from the least of them to the greatest. For I will forgive their wickedness and will remember their sins no more."* (Heb. 8:10-12) If we surrender all to God He will always be there for us. We would all have healing, we would all have strength, we would all have the glory that God has promised because in that Name we all have everlasting life!

CHAPTER 9

. . . And the Miracle Is — Always Being Ready

"No one knows about that day or hour, not even the angels in heaven, nor the Son, but only the Father. As it was in the days of Noah, so it will be at the coming of the Son of Man. For in the days before the flood, people were eating and drinking, marrying and giving in marriage, up to the day Noah entered the ark; and they knew nothing about what would happen until the flood came and took them all away. That is how it will be at the coming of the Son of Man. Two men will be in the field; one will be taken and the other left. Therefore keep watch, because you do not know on what day your Lord will come."
Matthew 24:36-42

Off in the distance there is a shadow of someone beckoning to me — I believe it is the Lord Jesus Christ calling. I realize how frightened I feel. I don't think I am ready to meet Him. Do I need more time? The true miracle of life is that if we surrender to Our Lord and Savior we will always be ready to be with Him. There will be no fear, but true joy, when He calls. Once we truly surrender our hearts to Him and live His will, we will always be prepared.

The best way to prepare for our encounter with Christ is by praying. I am reminded of a story written by a German poet by the name of Rilke. It seems a priest was out walking one day and he strolled past a cemetery. There a gravedigger was working very diligently. The priest stopped and began chatting with him. During the course of the conversation the gravedigger commented to the priest that he buried people in the ground, but the priest buried God in the sky. The priest was puzzled and asked him what he meant.

The gravedigger answered, ''Well, I'll explain. In the beginning of time, people prayed with their arms outstretched, their arms opened to God and God loved to throw Himself into all these human embraces, resting in their hearts. Then one day, a man who always prayed with open arms was nailed to a cross. Instead of being a symbol of openness, the outstretched arms became a symbol of suffering and pain. Consequently people began to pray with their hands folded, with their arms closed. They were afraid that if they were open they could be hurt. Even their churches, their buildings encouraged folded hands. Steeples were placed on top of the churches to symbolize folded hands pointing up to heaven. Their prayer, instead of being a prayer of openness, a prayer in which the Lord would throw Himself into hearts, became a prayer of pushing, poking and pleading — prayer for God to give them this and for God to give them that. The folded hands kept poking and poking and poking toward the sky, and it made God withdraw. God started to retreat. As the hands and the steeples kept getting higher and kept poking and pointing at God, God backed up so far that He fell out of the backside of heaven, into the darkness. God didn't mind the darkness though, because it reminded Him of human hearts. The human heart had become a very dark place." The gravedigger finished his explanation by saying, "That is why I say you have buried God in the sky and I bury people in the ground."

Stop and think — is this story typical of how we pray? Do our prayers poke and push God? Are they prayers of begging God to give me one thing or another? How often is my prayer open, allowing God into my heart? All too frequently that is my attitude. It is very easy to turn to God when there is trouble. Someone once said, "There are no atheists on the battlefield." It is true! On the battlefield of life when we are under the gun we look to God. It is very easy to say,

"God, I need this and I need that." It is so difficult to say, "God, I love you. Whatever you want for me I accept, because I know it is best," especially when we are still in pain, or still waiting to hear a good report from the doctor, or still hoping to find a job, or when we are at odds with those we love and feel neglected. I often wonder if I always remember to say even a quick "Thank you" when my prayer has been answered to my satisfaction. It is at those times I wish I would fling open my arms and praise Him, but it is rarely done.

Praying with outstretched arms is still so frequently a sign of pain and suffering, and yet prayer which leads us to a complete surrender to the Lord is the only way that we can really be ready for the final miracle of our lives — the ultimate healing when we are called to glory.

When I was learning about prayer in school I was told that there are four types — adoration, contrition, thanksgiving and supplication. "A.C.T.S." The acronym says it all! Once we pray and take Jesus into our heart, it is no longer what we say but how we act that becomes the real prayer in our life. The more we live the life of Jesus Christ, the more effective our prayers become. Every time we reach out to another person in kindness, we are adding a little bit of light to our heart.

The movie "E.T." illustrated what love does for the heart. Remember E.T.'s heart pulsed and glowed each time he was feeling love. It was a visible sign for all the world to see — so are ours. Our love changes the world. It does! It touches so many and then they touch so many and the world gets brighter and lighter. It is a beautiful thought — wherever we go we should turn on our heartlights. The more we turn on the lights in our hearts the more we are able to see that when God fell out of the backside of heaven into the darkness, it was into our hearts that He landed for *"God is love. Whoever lives in love lives in God, and God in him."* (1 John 4:16b)

In chapter 1 we spoke of a personal commitment to Jesus Christ as Lord and Savior of our lives. No one can make that for us — we must do it ourselves. Won't you take a few minutes now and commit your life to Jesus? It's a simple thing to do. Picture yourself in His presence. Open your arms wide and invite Him to fling Himself into your embrace. You may use your own words of acceptance or pray the following prayer — whichever you choose is fine — but invite Him in; don't let the moment pass.

A Prayer of Acceptance

Lord Jesus, I believe that you are the Christ, the Son of the living God. You have the Name above all names, the name which must be adored and revered for all time.

I come before you as a sinner in need of your mercy, confident that mercy will be mine. You died and rose again for the salvation of the whole world, and I thank you for allowing me to be part of that world.

I open my arms to your embrace and accept you as the personal Lord and Savior of my life. I renounce my sinfulness and all selfish actions and I rely totally on your strength as I journey towards the glory that you won for me.

Empower me by your Spirit to walk the path that you have marked out for me with the sure knowledge that if I fall or stray from the path, you will be there to help me. I accept the fact that you love me so much that you died for me as an individual.

I accept all that the Father created as good, and therefore I am lovable.

I accept the person that I am and rely totally on your strength to be the best that I can possibly be, fully realizing that all you ask is for me to try.

May I always show forth your goodness and love, bringing light to darkened hearts. May I safely reach Heaven to be with you for all eternity.

Come, Lord Jesus! Come into my life. I embrace you as my personal Lord and Savior. Come!

Epilogue

Over the years the one question that people have constantly asked me is, "Why have I not been healed? I've accepted Jesus as Lord and Savior of my life, I've prayed constantly, I have opened myself to the miracles of Jesus and yet I am still caught in the middle of my pain and suffering." There are no easy answers as to why God chooses to bestow physical healing on some and not on others. The thing we must remember is that the primary focus of healing should be spiritual. When Jesus walked this earth He did not totally eradicate illness and disease but He did by His death and resurrection win the victory over sin. This is the healing that all of us need in our lives. This is the healing He will give without hesitation once we have been born again.

Sometimes we might also wonder if indeed we have been born again. We have said the Acceptance Prayer and invited Jesus into our lives, but we don't know if He has really come. Our doubts tend to overwhelm us particularly when we don't see physical healing resulting from our prayers.

I think the easiest way for anyone of us to determine if the Spirit of Jesus is indeed present in our lives is by looking at the fruit that we show forth in our daily living. As I mentioned earlier Paul reminds us that the Fruit of the Spirit, ''love, joy, peace, patience, kindness, goodness, faithfulness, gentleness and self-control'' (Gal. 5:23-23), is present in the life of everyone who has accepted Jesus. We mustn't become too hard on ourselves and feel that because we don't have total peace or patience or kindness we don't have Jesus. Look to the example of an apple tree. Sometimes there is a late frost and some of the blossoms fall and the crop is nowhere near what we would like it to be. Nonetheless it is still an apple tree. That is the way it is in our lives — we might not always be as perfect as we would like but as long as we see the fruit we know that the spirit of God is there.

We can never take the presence of Jesus for granted. Like the fruit trees we must be nurtured and sometimes even pruned in order to make our fruit more abundant. Also, like the fruit trees if we neglect our spiritual life it will ultimately shrivel up and die. Read scripture and pray every day, and know beyond a shadow of a doubt that Jesus loves you more than you can imagine!

About the Author

Father John F. Campoli has been a priest in the Diocese of Trenton, New Jersey, since 1970. Father holds a master's degree in Theology from Mount St. Mary's Seminary, Emmitsburg, Maryland, and has pursued post graduate studies in Liturgy at Catholic University.

In addition to serving as both Parochial Vicar and Pastor of several parishes in the Trenton Diocese, Father also served as Director of Liturgy for the Diocese of Trenton for ten years. He has served on the Board of Directors of the Federation of Diocesan Liturgical Commissions. Father is presently Pastor of Holy Trinity Church, Long Branch, New Jersey.

For the past ten years Father Campoli has been involved in the Renewal and in the Healing Ministry. Father is a member of the Association of Christian Therapists. He is the Founder and Director of HIS LOVE MINISTRIES which is dedicated to spreading the news of the healing power of Jesus Christ.

Through his ministry, Father conducts healing Masses, Retreats and Days of Recollection both locally and abroad. Many people who have participated in prayer find both healing and peace in their lives. HIS LOVE MINISTRIES also embraces the newly formed "Catholic Women of Zion" — a statewide collective of approximately 200 women who meet monthly at the Berkeley Carteret Hotel, Asbury Park, New Jersey.